TWELVE DESERT FLOODS

TWELVE DESERT FLOODS

A Structural History of Egypt in Twelve Poems

by J. A. Gucci

Teacher Edition

Pressure System Press
New York, New York

2026

TWELVE DESERT FLOODS
A Structural History of Egypt in Twelve Poems—Instructor Edition

Published by Pressure System Press

First edition

ISBN: 978-1-972788-04-2

Printed in the United States

jagucci.com

Contents

How to Use This Book

This book presents Egyptian history through short poems organized around systems. Each poem models how a system operates, stabilizes, or repeats over time.

The poems are not meant to be interpreted in the traditional literary sense. Instead, they function as representations of structure. Each poem corresponds to a triad of related elements (for example: Flood · Silt · Renewal) that together describe how a system works.

The goal is not to ask what a poem "means," but to examine what the system does.

Each poem is paired with notes that provide:

- historical context
- a correspondence between the poem and a historical system
- discussion prompts aligned to the triad

These materials support observation, comparison, and analysis across contexts.

The poems may be used in a variety of settings:

- as brief openings to introduce a topic
- as points of comparison alongside historical material
- as prompts for discussion of cause and effect

• as models for describing systems in other domains

Because the poems are concise and focused, they can be incorporated into a lesson, seminar, or independent study without replacing existing material. They are intended to clarify structure rather than add interpretive complexity.

Across the book, attention should be given to repetition and stability. The systems presented here do not move toward a single outcome, but recur over time, sustaining the conditions of the civilization.

Man fears time,
but time fears the pyramids.
— Egyptian proverb

Instructor Notes

Poem Title: Inundation
Triad: Flood · Silt · Renewal

System Correspondence:

In ancient Egypt, the Nile River flooded annually, spreading water across the surrounding land. Unlike more variable river systems, this inundation followed a regular cycle. As floodwaters receded, they deposited nutrient-rich silt, creating fertile conditions for agriculture and long-term stability.

In the poem, the opening condition—"red brittle / jagged clay, / crushed mountains—"—establishes dry, hardened land prior to flooding. The shift occurs as water overtakes the land —"surge over banks— / broken"—marking the moment of inundation and transformation.

The movement—"splayed turtle-backs— / cattle on skiffs / drifting—"—reflects temporary submersion and displacement. The final image—"black mud"—corresponds to renewal: the fertile soil left behind as water recedes. This cyclical process sustained Egyptian agriculture and allowed the system to repeat over time.

Discussion Prompts:

Flood: What role does predictable flooding play in shaping an agricultural system?

Silt: How does the deposition of sediment alter the productivity of land?

Renewal: What results from a system that repeats and restores itself over time?

Inundation

Splayed turtle-backs—
cattle on skiffs
drifting.

Crushed mountain
surge over bank—
broken.

Red brittle
jagged clay—

black mud.

Instructor Notes

Poem Title: Threshing Floor
Triad: Field · Grain · Storage

System Correspondence:

In ancient Egypt, agriculture depended on the cultivation and harvesting of grain, especially wheat and barley. After harvest, grain had to be separated from husks and prepared for storage. These processes allowed food to be preserved and managed over time, supporting stability and planning.

In the poem, the opening condition—"drooping green / brown crown— / swollen tips"—establishes field: mature crops ready for harvest. The system begins with growth under stable environmental conditions.

The shift occurs as material is broken apart—"hurtling husks / plummeting"—corresponding to grain as a processed resource. Separation transforms what is grown into what can be collected and used.

The final image—"hummock"—corresponds to storage: gathered accumulation after processing. In Egypt, stored grain supported long-term food supply, enabling continuity and control across seasonal cycles.

Discussion Prompts:

Field: What conditions allow agricultural production to occur consistently?

Grain: How does processing transform crops into usable resources?

Storage: What results from the ability to preserve and manage food over time?

Threshing Floor

Drooping green
brown crown—
swollen tips.

Hurdling husks,
plummeting pines—

hummock.

Instructor Notes

Poem Title: Papyrus
Triad: Reed · Mark · Record

System Correspondence:

In ancient Egypt, papyrus plants growing along the Nile provided a material for writing. Stems were cut, pressed, and dried into sheets that could receive marks. This made it possible to record information, supporting administration, communication, and continuity over time.

In the poem, the opening condition—"black mud, / dust— / white spongy stem / curled, / leaning—"—establishes reed as the raw material emerging from a wet environment. The system begins with growth and availability.

The shift occurs as the plant is processed—"wide— / crushed rings"—corresponding to mark: the transformation of material into a surface capable of receiving and holding impressions.

The result is record—the ability to preserve marks across time. In Egypt, papyrus enabled systems of writing that supported organization, governance, and the transmission of knowledge.

Discussion Prompts:

Reed: What properties of papyrus made it suitable as a writing material?

Mark: How does processing a material allow it to carry information?

Record: What results from the ability to preserve information over time?

Papyrus

Black mud,
red dust—

white spongy stem
curled,
leaning—

wide—
crushed rings.

Instructor Notes

Poem Title: Mycelial Cord
Triad: Rope · Measure · Tax

System Correspondence:

In ancient Egypt, land was measured after the Nile flood to reestablish boundaries and assess agricultural production. These measurements formed the basis for taxation, allowing the state to track and collect resources. Systems of measurement made it possible to organize and extract value from the land.

In the poem, the opening condition—"braided bundles / fuzzy cords—"—establishes rope as a network of connection. Mycelial strands extend through soil, linking and organizing space.

The shift occurs as the network engages—"encoiling a root—" —corresponding to measure: the act of surrounding, assessing, and determining what is available within the system.

The final image—"white fan"—corresponds to tax: the outward collection and consolidation of resources. Like a ledger, the system gathers what has been measured and directs it toward a central point. In Egypt, measurement enabled taxation, supporting administration and state power.

Discussion Prompts:

Rope: What role do systems of connection play in organizing land or resources?

Measure: How does measuring make resources visible and accountable?

Tax: What results from the ability to assess and collect resources within a system?

Mycelial Cord

Braided bundles
fuzzy cords—

fused—
encoiling a root—

white fan.

Instructor Notes

Poem Title: Kill Site
Triad: Throne · Balance · Rule

System Correspondence:

In ancient Egypt, the pharaoh was understood as the central authority responsible for maintaining order, often described as balance (ma'at). This balance required active control over forces that could disrupt stability. Authority depended on the continual management of tension within the system.

In the poem, the opening condition—"scent and scratch marks — / rumbles, / carcass in a tree"—establishes throne: visible signs of dominance and control within a territory. Power is present and asserted.

The shift occurs as movement spreads—"scuttle— / rustle— / footprints in mud"—corresponding to balance: the system responding to disturbance. Activity extends beyond the initial act, creating instability that must be managed.

The final image—"ghost forest"—corresponds to rule: a condition where order is maintained despite underlying disruption. In Egypt, rule required continuous action to sustain balance within a system where disorder could emerge at any time.

Discussion Prompts:

Throne: What role does centralized authority play in establishing control within a system?

Balance: How do systems respond to disturbance or instability?

Rule: What results from the ongoing effort to maintain order over time?

Kill Site

Scent and scratch marks—
carcass
dragged up a tree.

Scuttle,
rustle,
footprints in mud—

ghost forest.

Instructor Notes

Poem Title: Fig Wasp
Triad: Temple · Offering · Priest

System Correspondence:

In ancient Egypt, temples functioned as sites where offerings were made and rituals were performed. These systems connected material contributions to structured processes carried out by designated roles. The continuity of the system depended on repeated cycles of offering and transformation.

In the poem, the opening condition—"wax green / cuticle— / bitter milk / white"—establishes temple as an enclosed, living structure. The fig forms a contained environment where the system operates.

The entry—"dusty wingless / wriggling— / wedged in lumen —"—corresponds to offering: the wasp enters the fig, bringing pollen and initiating the reproductive process. This action is necessary for the system to function.

The final condition—"gall"—corresponds to priest: a role embedded within the system that enables transformation. The wasp's body is broken down as part of the process, facilitating development within the enclosed structure. In Egypt, priests functioned within temple systems to carry out rituals that sustained continuity.

Discussion Prompts:

Temple: What role do enclosed or centralized spaces play in organizing systems?

Offering: How do inputs or contributions enable a system to function?

Priest: What roles emerge within a system to carry out and sustain its processes?

Fig Wasp

Wax green cuticle—
bitter white.

Dusty wingless
wriggling wasp

wedged in lumen—

gall.

Instructor Notes

Poem Title: Limestone
Triad: Stone · Labor · Monument

System Correspondence:

In ancient Egypt, limestone was a primary material for monumental construction, including temples and pyramids. These structures required the extraction, transport, and placement of massive stone blocks through coordinated labor. Over time, accumulated effort produced enduring architectural forms.

In the poem, the opening condition—"marine snow— / ooze — / alight on sea / floor"—establishes stone as accumulated biological material settling over time. The system begins with gradual deposition.

The shift occurs through pressure—"crushed— / plates under / plates—"—corresponding to labor: sustained force acting on material. Compression transforms soft accumulation into solid structure.

The final condition—"uplift— / mountain"—corresponds to monument: a large-scale form emerging from long-term accumulation and transformation. In Egypt, monuments similarly reflect the concentration of material and labor into enduring structures.

Discussion Prompts:

Stone: What processes allow material to accumulate into usable resources?

Labor: How does sustained effort transform material into structured form?

Monument: What results from the long-term accumulation of material and labor?

Limestone

Marine snow—
ooze—
alight on the sea
floor.

Plates under plates
crushed—
uplift—

mountain.

Instructor Notes

Poem Title: Root Wad
Triad: River · Boat · Trade

System Correspondence:

In ancient Egypt, the Nile functioned as a primary route for movement and exchange. Boats carried goods, materials, and people along the river, enabling trade and connection between regions. The flow of the river made transport possible, but also required points of interruption and gathering.

In the poem, the opening condition—"white water— / crests and breaks— / cutting a rock / bank"—establishes river as continuous movement. The system begins with flow and erosion.

The shift occurs as material enters and is caught—"leaf and litter— / pecked and pitted / log— / snagged"—corresponding to boat: an object carried within the current that becomes lodged. The log functions as a floating carrier of accumulated material.

The final condition—"gallery tunnels"—corresponds to trade: a system of redistribution that emerges from accumulation. Once caught, the log becomes a site of activity, supporting new forms of life and exchange. In Egypt, river transport similarly concentrated and redistributed resources along the Nile.

Discussion Prompts:

River: What role does continuous movement play in shaping systems of transport?

Boat: How do carriers enable the movement of materials within a system?

Trade: What results when resources are gathered, redirected, and redistributed?

Root Wad

White water—
crest and break—
cut rock
bank.

Leaflitter—
pecked and pitted
log—
snagged.

Gallery tunnels.

Instructor Notes

Poem Title: Chatter Marks
Triad: Bow · Chariot · War

System Correspondence:

In ancient Egypt, military systems depended on speed, coordination, and repeated force. Chariots enabled rapid movement across terrain, while archers delivered strikes in motion. Warfare involved sustained, repeated actions that reshaped the battlefield.

In the poem, the opening condition—"cracked boulder / settled on snow— / slope—"—establishes bow: stored potential energy within a system positioned for release. The condition is set for motion.

The shift occurs through movement—"bursting— / plucking —"—corresponding to chariot: force released and carried across a surface. Motion translates stored energy into repeated action.

The final condition—"polishing— / chatter marks"—corresponds to war: the accumulated result of repeated impacts. The surface is reshaped through continuous contact. In Egypt, warfare functioned through similar patterns of repeated force producing lasting change.

Discussion Prompts:

Bow: What role does stored energy play in initiating action within a system?

Chariot: How does movement carry and extend force across a landscape?

War: What results from repeated, sustained application of force?

Chatter Marks

Cracked boulder
settled in snow
slope—

bursting—
plucking—
polishing—

chatter marks.

Instructor Notes

Poem Title: Mycorrhiza
Triad: Mine · Tribute · Empire

System Correspondence:

In ancient Egypt, resources such as minerals were extracted from the environment and directed toward centralized authority. These materials supported construction, administration, and expansion. Systems of tribute ensured that resources flowed upward, reinforcing large-scale organization and growth.

In the poem, the opening condition—"acid— / liquid rocks / sucked through a root—"—establishes mine: extraction of material from the environment. The tree draws minerals from the soil, breaking down and absorbing what is otherwise inaccessible.

The exchange—"sugar— / braided pink / bundles of cords—" —corresponds to tribute: resources move between organisms in a structured relationship. The fungi receive sugars produced by the tree, forming a system of directed transfer.

The final condition—"acid…"—returns to continued extraction and expansion, corresponding to empire: a system that sustains itself through ongoing flows of resources. As the tree grows larger, it captures more light and expands its reach. In Egypt, systems of extraction and tribute similarly supported centralized growth and long-term stability.

Discussion Prompts:

Mine: What processes allow resources to be extracted from the environment?

Tribute: How do systems of exchange direct resources within a larger structure?

Empire: What results from sustained flows of resources through a system?

Mycorrhiza

Liquid rocks
sucked through a root—

sucked through a root—
sugar.

Braided pink
bundled cords—

acid—
liquid rocks…

Instructor Notes

Poem Title: Salinization
Triad: Drought · Invasion · Decline

System Correspondence:

In ancient Egypt, agricultural systems depended on the balance between fresh water and soil conditions. When water flow decreased or salts accumulated, soil productivity declined. Environmental changes could gradually reduce the ability of land to support crops, weakening the system over time.

In the poem, the opening condition—"landward / ocean waves under / river—"—establishes drought: reduced freshwater flow allows saltwater intrusion. The system begins to shift away from its previous balance.

The disruption—"sunken— / salted root reed / cuts a leaf—" —corresponds to invasion: salt enters the system and interferes with plant function. The intrusion alters internal processes and damages existing structures.

The final condition—"sulfur air"—corresponds to decline: the system degrades as conditions worsen. Productivity decreases, and the environment becomes less capable of sustaining life. In Egypt, similar processes could reduce agricultural output and destabilize local systems.

Discussion Prompts:

Drought: What conditions allow environmental balance to begin breaking down?

Invasion: How does the introduction of a disruptive element alter a system?

Decline: What results when a system's core conditions are degraded over time?

Salinization

Landward ocean
waves
under river.

Sunken—
salted root reed
cutting its leaf—

sulfur air.

Instructor Notes

Poem Title: Singing Dune
Triad: Tomb · Sand · Memory

System Correspondence:

In ancient Egypt, tombs were constructed to preserve the dead and maintain continuity beyond a single lifetime. These structures were embedded within desert landscapes, where shifting sand both concealed and protected what remained. Memory persisted not as fixed form, but through material traces shaped by the environment.

In the poem, the opening condition—"dune—"—establishes tomb: a formed structure within the landscape. The system begins with a defined but exposed presence.

The movement—"tumbling sand—"—corresponds to sand: constant motion that reshapes and reconfigures the surface. The structure is gradually covered, altered, and redistributed.

The final condition—"hum"—corresponds to memory: a resonance produced by movement rather than a visible form. The past persists as vibration and trace within the system. In Egypt, tombs functioned in this way, where preservation and erasure coexisted within the desert environment.

Discussion Prompts:

Tomb: What role do constructed spaces play in preserving continuity over time?

Sand: How does constant movement reshape and obscure existing structures?

Memory: What results when the past persists as trace rather than fixed form?

Singing Dune

Dune—

tumbling sand—

aeolian hum.

Guide to Use

This book presents Egyptian history through systems that repeat and stabilize over time. Each poem models a process that sustains continuity rather than producing a single outcome.

A typical use begins with close observation. The poem is read, and attention is directed toward condition, movement, and result. From there, the corresponding system can be identified and connected to historical material.

The poems may be used in a variety of ways:

- to introduce a topic through a recurring system
- to accompany historical readings as a parallel model
- to support discussion of stability and change
- to compare repeating systems across contexts
- to frame written or analytical responses

Because the poems are brief and focused, they can be incorporated into a lesson, seminar, or independent study without replacing existing material. They function as tools for recognizing pattern rather than as objects of interpretation.

Use may be adapted depending on context. The emphasis remains on identifying cycles, relationships, and the conditions that allow systems to persist over time.

Curriculum Placement

Typical Course Placement

This book aligns with courses that examine ancient Egypt, early civilizations, and long-term social and environmental systems.

It may be used within secondary or introductory postsecondary courses, as well as in interdisciplinary contexts that focus on continuity, structure, and human-environment interaction.

Curriculum Connections

The poems correspond to major themes in Egyptian history:

- river systems and agricultural cycles
- food production and storage
- systems of writing and record keeping
- political and religious organization
- resource management and distribution
- continuity, stability, and long-term development

Each poem models a system that reflects these conditions, allowing readers to examine how recurring processes sustain a civilization over time.

The material supports analysis of stability and change, comparison across systems, and the study of how long-term continuity is maintained.

Applied Exercise

This exercise approaches each poem as part of a repeating system.

Each poem may be treated as a record of a process that recurs over time. The task is to identify the system it represents and how it sustains continuity.

Working individually or in groups, select a poem and determine:

- what system is being modeled
- what process is repeating
- how the system maintains stability over time

For example:

A poem such as Inundation may be understood as:

condition → flood
process → deposition of silt
result → renewal of agricultural land

A poem such as Papyrus may be understood as:

material → reed
process → transformation into writing surface
result → preservation of information

After analysis, multiple poems may be arranged together. Viewed collectively, they form a set of interrelated systems that sustain a civilization through repetition and continuity.

The exercise may be adapted for discussion, written response, or comparative analysis. The emphasis remains on identifying recurring processes rather than interpreting symbolism.

Glossary

Inundation — the seasonal flooding of the Nile River

Silt — fine sediment deposited by water

Papyrus — a plant used to produce an early writing material

Threshing — the process of separating grain from husks

Mycelial — relating to a network of fungal threads

Tribute — resources directed to a central authority

Salinization — the accumulation of salt in soil

Limestone — sedimentary rock formed from compressed material

Chariot — a light vehicle used for rapid movement in warfare

Dune — a mound of sand shaped by wind

Appendix

The Triad Method

The poems in this book are organized around triads—groups of three related elements that describe how a system operates.

Rather than presenting history as a sequence of events, the triads focus on relationships between conditions, actions, and outcomes. Each triad represents a process: a system that forms, stabilizes, or changes over time.

A triad may be understood as:

condition → what exists
interaction → what acts upon it
result → what emerges

The poems model these relationships using observable processes. The goal is not to interpret the poem, but to identify how the system functions.

This method can be applied beyond the book. Any system—historical, ecological, or social—can be examined by identifying three interacting elements that explain how it operates.

By focusing on structure rather than description, the triads provide a way to see how complex systems develop and persist over time.

The Twelve Series

Each book in this series presents systems through short, structured poems.

Rather than describing events, the poems model how systems form, operate, and persist over time.

Each volume focuses on a different historical context while using the same underlying method. Together, they show how similar patterns appear across different environments and societies.

The books may be read individually or as a sequence. Viewed together, they reveal how systems develop, stabilize, interact, and transform across time.

History

Mesopotamia — Formation
Greece — Interaction
Rome — Expansion and Collapse
Medieval — Thresholds

Creative Writing

Twelve Small Windows
Twelve Loops
Twelve Mirrors
Twelve Rooms

Philosophy

Twelve Iron Paradoxes

Colophon

This book was set in a clear, readable typeface to support close observation and sustained attention.

The poems follow a consistent structure to emphasize pattern, change, and system relationships.

Designed and produced as part of the Twelve series.

www.ingramcontent.com/pod-product-compliance
Ingram Content Group UK Ltd.
Pitfield, Milton Keynes, MK11 3LW, UK
UKHW042011190726
13854UKWH00005B/2241